KB113933

본서의 한글 해석본은 www.yjbooks.com
에서 다운로드 받을 수 있습니다.

KBS Cool FM 굿모닝팝스와 함께하는

Great Koreans
Father TAESUK LEE

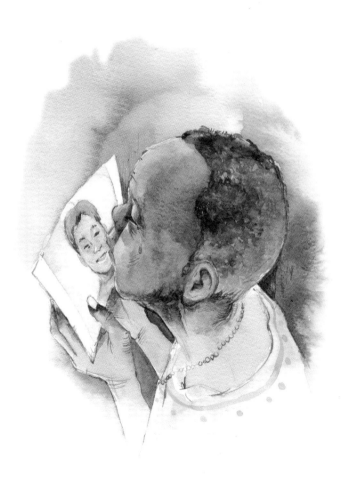

KBS Cool FM 굿모닝팝스와 함께하는 Great Koreans

Father TAESUK LEE

The Greatest Love of All

KBS Cool FM 굿모닝팝스, Celine Kim 지음

영진미디어

KBS Cool FM 굿모닝팝스와 함께하는
Great Koreans
Father TAESUK LEE

초판 1쇄 인쇄 2011년 10월 25일
초판 1쇄 발행 2011년 10월 30일

지은이   KBS Cool FM 굿모닝팝스, Celine Kim
펴낸이   이준경
펴낸곳   (주)영진미디어
출판 등록   2011년 1월 7일 제141-81-22416

주소   경기도 파주시 교하읍 문발리 504-3 파주출판단지 영진미디어 사옥
전화   031-955-4955
팩스   031-955-4959
이메일   book@yjmedia.net
홈페이지   www.yjbooks.com
디자인   디자인허브
종이   삼승페이퍼
출력   하람커뮤니케이션
인쇄   광문인쇄사

값 10,000원
ISBN 978-89-965772-5-6

· 저자와의 협의에 따라 인지는 생략합니다.
· 이 책은 저작권법에 의해 보호를 받는 저작물이므로 무단전재와 복제를 금합니다.
· 이 책에 언급된 모든 상표는 각 회사의 등록 상표입니다.
  또한 인용된 사이트의 저작권은 해당 사이트에 있음을 알려드립니다.
· 잘못된 책은 본사나 구입하신 서점에서 교환해드립니다.

이 책은 '영어로 읽는 위대한 한국인' 시리즈입니다. 초등학교 고학년에서 중학생까지 읽기에 적당한 수준이며, 뒤쪽으로 갈수록 어휘가 다양해집니다. **12세~15세 청소년** 대상의 **TOEFL Junior**를 준비하고 있는 학생들이 보기에 적절합니다.

초등학교 고학년			중학생		
11세	12세	13세	14세	15세	16세
	←			→	

기준	난이도
단어	2000 단어 내외
문법	시제를 구분하고 구와 절의 문장 구조를 이해할 수 있는 정도
독해	글을 읽고 정확한 내용을 파악하여, 질문에 답하거나 다음 내용을 추론할 수 있는 종합적인 사고력을 지닌 정도

※ 청담 어학원의 Tera, Bridge, Par 레벨, 토피아 어학원의 HT4, GB, G1 레벨, 아발론 어학원의 JB, JI, JA 레벨 정도의 학생들이 보기에 적절합니다.

가장 위대한 것은 사랑입니다

이태석 신부가 운명하고 저희 가족은 큰 상실감을 겪었습니다. '왜 하느님께서는 온몸을 바쳐 사랑을 실천하며 산 이태석 신부를 그렇게 일찍 데려가셨는가?'라는 의문도 들었습니다. 그러나 시간이 지날수록 '하느님께서는 이태석 신부가 가장 아름다울 때 데려가기를 원하셨구나'라는 생각이 점점 더 강하게 듭니다.

이태석 신부가 숨을 거둔 후 저의 첫마디는 "태석아, 미안해!"였습니다. 같은 수도사제로서의 길을 걸어가면서 사랑을 위해 온몸을 다 바친 그의 삶 앞에 제 자신이 부끄러웠기 때문입니다. 그러면서 한편으로는 사랑을 위해 모든 것을 불태울 수 있었던 그의 삶이 부러웠습니다. 기도할 때마다 사랑의 삶을 다짐하면서도 그렇게 살지 못하는 나 자신의 삶이었기 때문입니다.

이태석 신부의 삶이 우리에게 전해주는 가장 큰 메시지는 사랑의 위대함입니다. 『울지마, 톤즈!』를 제작한 구수환 PD의 말처럼 세상을 변화시키는 더 큰 힘은 세상의 불의에 대한 비판과 고발보다 사랑이라는 것을, 이태석 신부는 자신의 삶과 죽음을 통해 우리에게 보여주었기 때문입니다. 이태석 신부가 우리에게 마지막으로 남긴 말도 "하느님은 정말 사랑이십니다."였습니다.

꿈을 이루기 위해 노력하십시오. 이태석 신부와 함께 살았던 가족으로서 드리고 싶은 말씀은 이태석 신부도 우리 곁에 살았던 한 사람이라는 것입니다. 다만 우리와 달랐던 점은 자신이 믿었던 바대로 살겠다고 결심을 했고, 그 결심한 것을 실천했다는 것입니다. 이태석 신부가 걸어갔던 길이 불가능한 길은 아니라고 생각합니다. 결심을 하고 그 결심을 실천하기 위해 많은 노력을 해야 하기에 선뜻 그 길을 가지 못할 뿐이라고 생각합니다. 부디 우리 청소년들이 아름다운 것과 올바른 것을 꿈꾸고, 그렇게 살아 제2의, 제3의 이태석 신부가 나오기를 간절히 기도드립니다.

이태영 신부님(이태석 신부님의 형)

CONTENTS

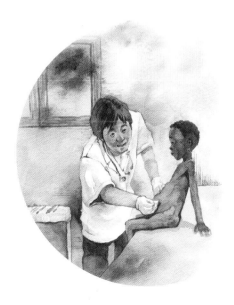

Don't Cry for Me, Tonj

February 2010, Tonj - a small village in Sudan and one of the most isolated areas of the country. The main tribe in Tonj is 'Dinka.' The people of Dinka usually fight back tears in their tradition. They consider it shameful to show tears to anyone other than oneself. Yet they mourned openly in tears for the death of Taesuk Lee with all their hearts. Among the saddened hearts, the brass band children were the most devastated because they loved and cherished him so much. He was the only person who implanted a future to hope and dream for.

"We have yet to tell him, 'thank you.' "

They could not stop crying, knowing they would never see him again. Calming down, they sang together the song that Father Lee had taught them.

I love you. I love you from the bottom of my heart.
I can't possibly count all of my tears that I shed
when you left me .

The band members agreed to give him a last gift in appreciation. They played music, marching in a procession toward the church, the place for his funeral service. At the very front of the band walked a few boys holding his pictures. People started to gather around the parade.

"Father Jolie!" they shouted. Jolie is the local nickname for John Lee, Lee's English name.

The pictures reminded them of his sacrifices. They expressed their thanks toward his pictures and kept him company during his last journey of this world by following the parade.

Younger Days, Warm and Gifted

Taesuk Lee was born in Busan on September the 19th, 1962. He was the ninth of ten children. His mother survived her husband when he was ten, and had to raise her children alone. She made her living by her needle, working at a big and crowded fish market. She worked day and night to earn food for one day. Though she was busy and worn out, she was able to gain strength to see her lovely and bright children.

Taesuk was a special boy for his mother. He was mature and considerate for his age. Far from acting like a child, he put his heart into what he should do. Not just studying hard, but also helping his mother with the housework because he wanted to bring smiles to his mother's face.

"Mom, let me carry that bundle of clothing for you."

"Thanks, Taesuk. You really are a kind person, but I feel happier when you work on what you should do for now."

To her wish, he did well in all schoolwork. He was often at the top of the whole school. He liked math. He enjoyed the sense of satisfaction it brought, after having finished challenging problems. He picked up his award and hurried back to his mom.

"Wow, you've done a great job! I'm so proud of you."

He was so pleased to see his mom's smile. And he put even more efforts into everything he did.

Taesuk's mother was a devout Catholic. She took her ten children together to mass every Sunday. Taesuk loved going to church. Everything in the church - praise songs of the choir,

sermons of the priest, priestly robes, and even solemn silence sweeping across inside of the chapel - struck his fancy. It was in church where Taesuk found peace and a sense of bliss.

One day he was attending a mass when he was struck by some words from the priest.

"Jesus said, 'I tell you the truth, whatever you did for one of the least of these brothers of mine, you did for me.'"

Those words of God tugged at the strings of his heart. He could not stop thinking of them as he went home. They even rang in his ears in bed. They eventually turned out to have the greatest impact on his life. He made up his mind to live according to what Jesus said.

"I want to live for the poor and weak," he said to himself.

Immediately he put his thoughts into practice. He went to the House of the Sisters of Mary, an orphanage located near his village. Some of the children at the House had lost their parents and the others had been deserted. He was moved by the sisters taking care of the children as if they were their own. He and the orphans soon got on like a house on fire. He enjoyed hanging out with them so much that he sometimes failed to return home. He forgot to pay attention to what his elder brother had told him.

"Hey, Taesuk, if you get back home late, you worry Mom."

His mother's concerned look came to his mind all at once. Hesitatingly, he said goodbye to his friends and left for home. The sisters were proud that he had such a warm heart.

He found so much passion in the work of caring for the orphans that he wanted to keep on doing the same thing.

"I wish to build an orphanage. I sense that's what I'm called to do," he said to his sister.

He gradually built up his heart for the poor and weak in this way.

The church held a little event one day. Taesuk and his family were getting ready for the event. They got dressed up. In fact, they always took special care in getting dressed when going to church. They believed this was the best honor they could give to Jesus. On the way to the church, Taesuk noticed some boys in the neighborhood making fun of a little beggar.

"Look at that! They are dressed in rags. Hey, beggars, beggars!"

The little beggar was dressed in old and shabby clothes that needed mending. The scene he just witnessed broke his heart. He rebuked the mocking boys and headed to the boutique where his sister was working. He snatched up thread and needles and scurried to the beggar kid. He set about fixing the old clothes. His clumsy but careful work moved the kid's heart, and he felt much better.

"Wow, this looks just like new clothes."

"Sure, it does. From now on, you tell me whenever you have any clothes to fix. OK?"

Feeling better on his part, Taesuk headed for the church with the kid.

In addition to reading books, He was fond of music. He loved going to the top of the mountain which his village nestled on. That was the place where he had the happiest moments of all. He could sing aloud while looking down on the coast of Busan.

He became familiar with notes singing praise songs in the hymnbooks. Music was a good friend of his. He also showed an exceptional talent for music. He even sang in a competition and won an award in it. He served as a soprano member of the choir at the church he attended when he was an elementary school student.

"You have a beautiful and high-pitched voice, so you fit for the soprano part," acclaimed the priest.

His pure and clear voice touched the hearts of a lot of people attending the mass.

He learned how to write songs and sing a solo from the music teacher at his junior high school. He was a fast learner going way beyond his teacher's expectations. His gift and attitude pleased her so much that she put extra efforts into teaching him. With her guidance, Taesuk learned to compose many beautiful songs. And he even earned awards at several song contests.

He was also good at playing musical instruments. He loved every instrument he came upon including the clarinet, saxophone and flute. To him, they were the fulfillment of complete musical harmony bringing him comfort and peace of mind. Whenever he saw a new instrument, he practiced it day and night. Most of the time, alone. It sometimes seemed that he showed little improvement, but he refused to give up. After a while he finally found himself skilled at playing it.

He had a special favor for pianos. He fell in love with them at first sight. He was on the way home the day when he first heard the piano sound. The sound flowing from the corner of the street dazzled him.

'Ah, I want to learn to play the piano.'

He was eager to learn to play the piano although his family could afford neither the instrument nor a mentor. At that time the piano was an expensive instrument to learn - barely one or two households in his whole neighborhood owned one. Lee's mother was already having a hard time paying for ten tuition fees. Nevertheless, Taesuk did not yield to the situation.

'Oh, the church has an organ. I can practice with it!'

He dashed toward the church and found the organ, shining in the sunlight. From then on, he rushed to the church after school and practiced the organ with the hymnbooks. The organ was placed right on the spot where the sunlight was beaming its golden rays. And mysteriously enough, Jesus on the cross looked as if He was directly gazing on it. Taesuk sensed a warm feeling not only due to the sunlight but also Jesus' look - graceful moments of Jesus' love toward a poor boy.

As time went by, he acquired enough skill to play hymns. The choirmaster, impressed with his improvement, entrusted him to play for the children's choir. Before long, he also took charge in playing for the adult choir during official mass.

Furthermore, he had an exceptional ability in writing songs. He composed children's praise songs such as "Christmas," "The Round Sun," and "Little Stars."

He was also outstanding in the choir team. He exercised such an active leadership that the members willingly followed him as a competent leader. During the church festivals, he directed drama performances apart from singing and acting himself, and was successful each time. People liked all that he put his efforts into, and he was thrilled to see them enjoy it.

'My musical gift can make people happy.'

He thanked Jesus for His gracious gift.

Deciding to Become a Priest

One day Taesuk watched a movie called *The Story of Saint Damien* at the church. He could not leave his seat even long after the movie ended. His brother found him in tears.

"It was so touching."

The Story of Saint Damien deals with the life of a Catholic priest in the 19th century who dedicated his life to lepers in Molokai, a little island near Hawaii. At the Kalaupapa National History Park in Hawaii, a cross stood in commemoration of his works.

"Greater love has no one than this, that he lay down his life for his friends," it says on the cross.

Taesuk deeply reflected on his life.

'Will I be able to live like him?'

Since then he desired to become a priest and live a sacrificial life for people in need.

In 1981, he graduated from high school and entered medical school. He wanted to go to the seminary to become a priest. But, his mother opposed. His older brother, Taeyoung, had already entered seminary before him, and his older sister was involved in the church ministry. Two of her children giving their lives to God was enough she thought.

"My son! You don't have to be a priest. You're an intelligent person. You can be the light of the world without being a priest. Besides, you can cure a lot of sick people if you become a doctor."

Being a good son to her as always, he obeyed his mother.

"Alright, I'll be a doctor and cure sick people."

He was admitted to Inje University Medical School. He studied very hard to become a doctor. He went on to build his career as an army surgeon. As he always did, he took good care of the people there. In his spare time, he regularly visited a small church near the military compound. He soon became a close friend to the priest. Sometimes he would doze off or fall into a sound sleep at the priest's office. At those moments, he felt like being at one with the church. He recalled an old desire that had been kept in him for a long time.

"I want to be a priest!"

It seemed to him that Jesus had sent him to the church. He sensed His calling more strongly than ever before. That was not to say that he lost his interest for serving as a doctor. On the contrary, he still loved the job. But nothing gave him more happiness than being at church. He said to his brother Fr.

Taeyoung.

"I want to be a priest like you."

Hearing this, Fr. Taeyoung tried to persuade him earnestly.

"Living a priest's life is nothing like living a safe and sure life. You need to give up a lot of things."

"I know, and I've already made up my mind."

"Well, you need to convince your mom first."

So Taesuk went to see his mother, and said the words he had been longing to say.

"Mom, I really can't give up on being a priest."

"But Taesuk, you are almost ready to be a professional doctor."

"Sorry, Mom. I wanted to make money and let you live in comfort. But..."

"Can you reconsider? We already have two people devoted to God."

"I can't picture my life without being a priest. Unless I

live as a priest, my life is meaningless."

She began to weep. Soon her face was full of tears. She felt for her son. Taesuk wept, too.

She eventually decided to respect his decision. He joined Salesian Brothers, a Catholic order with the mission of caring and educating underprivileged youths. It was not a difficult choice for him. He had a heart for the underprivileged for a long time. He then entered Gwangju Catholic University, and pursued his studies further in Rome, Italy. He was ordained as a deacon at Rome in 2000 and then as a priest on the 24th of June, 2001, at the age of forty.

The Encounter with Tonj - Destiny

It was summer in 1999 when Taesuk was still studying in Rome. He joined a mission team for Africa. His heart started to flutter. He looked forward to visiting the area because he was eager to help people living in undeveloped countries. The first place the team went was Nairobi, Kenya. Nairobi was a large, economically-developed city. Taesuk did not feel any passion for serving in that region. The team went to the next site-Tonj, Sudan. Taesuk was shocked to see things he had never seen before.

"Oh, God. This is too much."

Sudan was at war. Villages were desolate and run-down with shattered houses. People seemed to be in the worst condition on the earth. People were skin and bones, some with no arms or legs, scrawny little kids doing nothing all day, and women walking for hours for water. The worst of all was a village of lepers. They had wounds covering their entire body and had lost their sense of touch. A stench rose from the village because of their festering wounds. They were deserted people, which left them deep scars. They suffered from unconcern and indifference as well as poverty.

Taesuk wanted to be with them. He recalled a word of God that he had cherished since he was young.

"Jesus said, 'I tell you the truth, whatever you did for one of the least of these brothers of mine, you did for me.'"

'Oh, Tonj and its people were the least of all!'

He also remembered the movie, *The story of Saint Damien*.

'I want to live as Saint Damien.'

He made himself a promise to come back to Tonj after ordination.

In a plane to Tonj, in December 2000, Taesuk reflected on the past few days. He was thinking about when he announced his plan to his family. He was excited to have a new life in Tonj, but was still worrying about leaving them.

"I've decided to go on a mission to Sudan."

None of his family received his announcement favorably.

"We have a lot of people in need in Korea."

"Why do you insist on going to a tough place like that?"

Taesuk was firm and determined.

"Because nobody wants to go there. They need me."

His mother found herself in tears, but she did not want to get in the way of her son's purpose. So she stopped thinking of her own desire, and no longer tried to discourage him. She finally let him go. And since then, she never missed even a single day in going to the early morning prayer service to pray for him.

Sudan, together with Somalia, is the poorest country in Africa. It won its independence from English colonial rule in 1956. The Arabs in the north forced out the native peoples in the area to the southern region. Now Sudan is divided into two: North Sudan with Islamic Arabs, and South Sudan with the original people of the land. They are Christians, and Tonj belongs to this area. Not much later, a large amount of oil deposits were found in the southern region. People of the North started to attack the Southern people. And so, the people took up arms to defend themselves. The war between the two regions lasted for 23 years. Over 2,000,000 people died during the conflict.

Under the rule of England, the North had seen a great advancement with cities, roads, schools, and hospitals. On the other hand, the South had seen nothing but endless barren lands. And now, the Arabs cut all the supply routes to the South. Without any food and necessities, the people of the South began to starve to death. They started to point guns at each other. Cows and women, more than anything else, were the reason behind the bloody fighting. The conflicts occurred between tribes and even within families. Countless people were injured or killed. The area quickly turned into hell on earth.

People in the South traveled as far as Nairobi, Kenya for the things they need to survive. This region is over 2,000 km away. The roads were too poor to travel on. They were unpaved and full of mud pits caused by heavy rainfall. Cars could only travel no more than 20 to 30 km/h. In the rainy season, the roads turn into complete mud, isolating the area completely. Without any electricity, TV, telephone, or the Internet, South Sudan becomes an area disconnected from the outside world. There, one would never know what is happening outside.

Fr. Taesuk Lee was ordained as a priest in Korea, in June 2001 and sent to Kenya in October of the same year. And it was two months later in December he reached Tonj and devoted himself to the missionary work there. Fr. Taesuk started his mission in Tonj amongst the horrible conditions. However, people should not be judged by their appearances. In his first impression, Tonj was a dangerous and desolate place with a poor population. But as time passed, he began to discover a beauty that he had never seen before. Not only a beauty, but a fullness.

One day, he went to a hospital to check up on a boy with malaria. He was with his father, and seemed to be in an argument with him. He was holding a bowl of corn soup in his hand.

"Is there anything I can do to help?" Fr. Taesuk asked.

"Father, I told my dad to share this bowl, and he keeps refusing to," the boy replied.

The dad was in desperate need to nurse his little child. They stood staring at each other for a while, and finally confirmed their love for each other.

'What a beautiful scene!'

A beautiful heart to share the few things they have. A beautiful heart to find happiness in the few things they have. They were truly rich people.

Fr. Taesuk was even more moved by the lepers who were in much more miserable conditions than ordinary Tonj people. One day Fr. Taesuk was handing out a monthly ration of corn and vegetable oils. This was used to make a bowl of porridge. Suddenly, a woman approached him with her little daughter.

"Look, doctor. I think she's got the disease."

So he examined spots on her body.

"Don't worry. These are just from a simple fungus."

He tried to reassure her while she had a very sad look on her face. He was curious and was later told that she hoped her daughter had leprosy. If her daughter had leprosy, she would be able to get extra corn and oils.

'She wants her own child to get the disease to get food for
her family? Her heart must be completely broken.'

Fr. Taesuk felt such compassion that he went to her where
she lived and gave extra corn and oils.

The lepers had never had medical treatment before. Until
now, they just lived in their pain. Fr. Taesuk touched their hands
and feet and started to gently tend to their wounds. He squeezed
the pus, applied medicine, and dressed the wounds carefully.
More and more people came to see him to receive treatment.
Physically worn out, he kept tending to them. He learned to
communicate with them, and his love towards them increased.

Fr. Taesuk Lee was seeking to do something special for them
when he noticed their bare feet. He placed each of their feet,
some deformed and even some toeless, on sheets of paper to
draw their shapes. He then recorded the names of each person,

and brought the paper home to make customized sandals for each of them. On Christmas Eve, he took the sandals he had made to their village, and he himself put them on each person. In this way he had given each of the lepers their first time ever Christmas gift, which also happened to be their first time ever one and only custom-made pair of shoes.

Meanwhile, his first impression of them changed. He used to regard them as poor people. But later, he began to see an amazing power in them. One day, a leper from the village dropped in on him.

"This is a chicken I'm raising. Make soup out of it, and you'll like it."

Fr. Taesuk said, "Are you really giving me this?"

Fr. Taesuk was astonished at what he had just heard. In fact, a chicken was one week's worth of food for one family. Rarely had he been given any thanks in other villages. But here in Tonj, a person from the most miserable of conditions came to him to say thank you. He realized that they were the richest people in the world, even though they had no health or property. The people of Tonj were the encouragement and power for him to keep serving them. As if by magic, he found himself restored whenever he was with them. He liked being with them.

'We believe that the more we get, the happier we will be.'

He reflected on himself and repented of his wrong views. He also thanked God for sending him off there to teach him this valuable lesson. From time to time when he visited Korea, he wondered at how much he had changed. He was pleased with every little thing including a glass of water and a long-distance bus. He was a person who had learned to know how to thank for every little thing.

Tonj is a non-industrialized area. Not a single factory can be found there. Yet, it has wonderful nature. God's artistic ability often amazed Fr. Taesuk. Tonj is also filled with clean air that could only be found deep in the mountains. No smoking chimneys and no cars fuming out exhaust. Tonj has a vast, open plain. Monkeys and deer walk or run across the plain. Birds of passage occasionally stop to rest. Countless unknown butterflies flit from flower to flower. Further, Tonj has naturally muddy roads. As cars must go slow, no one gets hurt or dies from traffic accidents. Human beings live in harmony with the surrounding animals and plants.

"How beautiful this is!" Fr. Taesuk exclaimed.

Still, the big, clear eyes of the children were more impressive to him than anything else.

"Here in Sudan, we have two things hard to find in Korea. One is an immeasurable number of stars in the night sky, and the other is the big pure eyes of the children, which seem ready to burst any moment. I am so deeply saddened to see such big eyes. But then I begin to look at them in admiration, and sense God is somewhere in there deeply hidden. It reminds me that all humans are God's creation."

It was on the 24th of May, 2001 - a year after Fr. Taesuk came to Tonj, and the Day of Solemnity. People decorated the statue of the Virgin Mary with wild flowers, and were having their first ever parade. The procession just approached the center of the village when there was a roaring sound heard from a plane. It was 'Antinop,' a scary bomber. It had dropped bombs all over the country during the war and killed many people. It usually creates a terrible noise which draws inherent fear from the people. The people instantly lie down on the ground upon hearing the noise. Often times it goes away and comes back even before they can breathe a sigh of relief, causing them to further panic.

"It's Antinop!" they shouted.

People were glued to where they were, wishing for it to keep going by. Against their wish, it turned back. It was just ready to drop bombs.

Surprisingly, people reacted differently than usual. Instead of running away in panic, they put the statue down on the ground and then themselves. They did not want to leave it behind. The statue was standing still. It appeared to watch over its people. At last, Antinop started to release the bombs. One, two, three... fourteen in all. Then, a mysterious thing happened; all the bombs deviated from the village, as if driven by some mysterious force. People were watching the scene with puzzled amazement. Finally, Antinop was gone.

"The Virgin Mary created a miracle!" uttered people.

"She protected us!"

There would be no better explanation than this. They just witnessed the love of God towards them. Since that day, the Solemnity became a special day for them as well as for Fr. Taesuk. Fr. Taesuk felt God's special love and purpose for him also.

'Indeed I did not come here by my will, but His will. He called me to be His hands and feet and to serve these suffering people.'

He became assured of His calling.

'Ah, Tonj has always been His plan for me. It's my destiny!'

Becoming a Doctor - the Most Needed
One for the Poor

There was only one clinic in Tonj. It did not function well because of a lack of doctors. People had to endure the pain. Heat, unclean water, and ignorance caused the infectious disease to spread. Many people even dropped dead without knowing what had killed them. Fr. Taesuk decided to be a doctor as soon as he arrived in Tonj. He could not let people die any longer. Fortunately, he had already obtained a medical degree.

The first work that he undertook was to build a new clinic.

The previous clinic consisted of a roof woven with dry weeds and bamboo poles. It had no electric facilities. He had a hard time examining patients. Rooms inside were low and narrow. He always had to bend forward and down to enter. There was no drug storage, which might cause a serious problem since drugs need to be kept at a constant temperature. There was no room for patients, either. They had to be placed on the straw bed, which made them vulnerable to further infection.

"I can't keep treating patients under these conditions."

He made up his mind to build a new place for treatment. But then, he faced a problem. There were not enough materials to build anything in Tonj. He changed his original plan to use cement, and designed another plan. He started to use local materials instead.

'Tonj is abundant in mud. I should use it.'

He baked bricks out of mud and built walls with them. He then covered the top with tin plates. The one side of the roof was made of transparent plastic so that it could absorb sunlight. In this way the building was bright enough to examine patients without electricity. The building was also made tall enough to allow people to stand upright at the entrance.

Three years later, he made the big decision to renovate the building with cement. He, together with the villagers, worked hard to collect sand. It was sweaty work under the blazing sun. What was worse, they had to travel as far as Nairobi, Kenya in order to get other materials. This was even harder than putting up the building. They sometimes faced situations that seemed impossible to get the necessary materials. But Fr. Taesuk never gave up. He paid extra to get them no matter what. With their efforts and commitment, the new clinic was finally built. It was equipped with twelve rooms including a doctor's office, examination room, injection room, patient's room, drug storage, and a staff room for volunteers. It was a huge advancement for the people of Tonj. Fr. Taesuk was so proud of them.

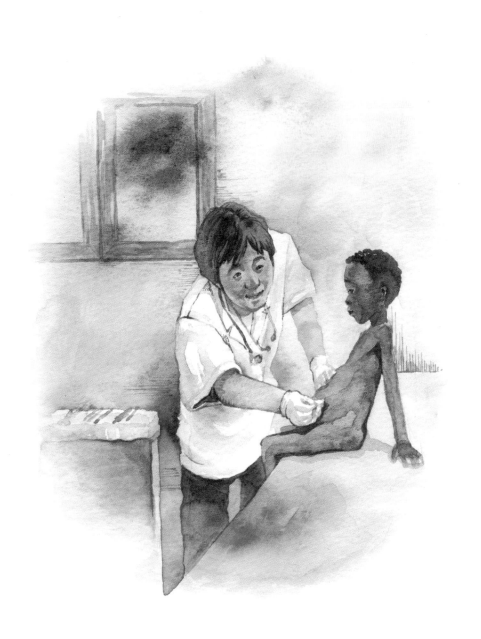

It was not easy to take care of patients under the poor conditions. One of the hardest things that Fr. Taesuk had to deal with was infectious diseases. One day, cholera broke out and swept through the village. It was due to unclean water. People had large and small wars for 25 years, and so there was no time to build water-purifying systems. Fr. Taesuk wanted to dig wells and install manual pumps, but it did not work due to a lack of resources. So the people drank river water polluted with worms, sand, and animal droppings, which became the major reason behind cholera. Cholera spread like wildfire. Once one member of the family got the disease, the entire family would also get it.

"Father, help me!"

People were standing in a long queue outside of the clinic building. The front yard of the building was overcrowded with patients lying down. Fr. Taesuk attended to them without eating or drinking, but the situation went out of control. The number of patients kept increasing. Cholera is fatal to humans. Once it gets into the human body, it causes vomiting and diarrhea. And eventually, it makes the patients die of dehydration one or two hours after they get the disease.

He kept on giving the patients infusions, but people kept dying under his very nose. He had to do something. He asked the students to help him.

"Guys, help me. Just give infusions next to me."

With several helpers who can give infusions to the dehydrated, he could save a lot of lives. The students were afraid, though.

"But we could be infected in that way."

"Yes, we don't want to die yet."

He understood how they felt, but he thought that it was more important to save lives than to think about one's own feelings. Also, he was being an example himself.

"God helps those who do His work. So don't worry."

His earnest request moved their hearts. They decided to do

the work after all.

"First, you must never touch your mouth with your hands. Second, you must wash your hands with an antiseptic cleanser. Always keep these two things in mind."

They tried hard to help him. He took pride in their devotion to saving people.

The disease began to die down. For one whole month everyone worked hard to fight the disease.

'If they had been aware of how to prevent cholera, they wouldn't have lost so many lives.'

As a matter of fact, a lot of people did not go to see the doctor, mistaking the disease for just diarrhea. They did not even know that the river water is not suitable for drinking. Fr. Taesuk refused to yield to ignorance.

'From now on, I will inform them of my medical knowledge as much as I can to help prevent diseases,' thought Fr. Taesuk.

He thanked God for having equipped him with such

knowledge.

Fr. Taesuk faced many difficult times because of 'Kujur,' a shaman and sorcerer. People believed whatever he said - a kind of superstition. People went to see Kujur whenever they were ill. Later, they would come to the clinic after the disease became worse. Some died before anything could be done because they believed exactly what Kujur had said.

Once, a seven-year-old girl, the daughter of a nurse, was brought into the hospital in the middle of the night. After examining her, Fr. Taesuk diagnosed her illness. She had malaria. But it wasn't sure why she had fits. He performed the treatment for malaria, but the convulsions grew stronger. Her parents told him that they would bring her to the Kujur.

"This child would surely die if you bring her to Kujur," said Fr. Taesuk.

He persuaded the nurse to give him thirty more minutes. He

then administered the malaria medicine to her again. After a while, the convulsions stopped and she fell into a sound sleep. He breathed a sigh of relief.

"Thank you so much, Father."

Her parents were also relieved. Fr. Taesuk shuddered to think of them going to Kujur.

'What if they had gone to Kujur?'

On another occasion, a son of the chief of a tribe was carried into the hospital. He showed a sign of paralysis; he gazed blankly, and could not speak a word.

"How long has he been like this?"

"For a month."

"Why didn't you bring him earlier?"

"We went to see all the best Kujurs and they even performed exorcisms, which didn't work. This place is our last hope."

"Oh, God..."

Fr. Taesuk concluded that the son had meningitis, and treated him with every means possible. Still, he was not sure if the son could recover from the illness. Already a whole month had passed by. Two weeks later though, the son started to move, speak, and even swallow food. One month later, he was fully recovered and ready to be discharged.

"I'm so grateful to you."

His father, the chief, presented Fr. Taesuk with a couple of bulls in gratitude for his care. In fact, the Dinka tribe seldom expresses thanks to anybody except for some special days. Fr. Taesuk felt proud and fulfilled. Finally, he thought he could gain trust from the tribesmen.

Eighty to ninety percent of the patients whom he took care of suffered from malaria. This was the most common disease in Tonj. Fr. Taesuk now became a specialist in malaria. He was even able to determine the symptom of the patients simply by watching their walking posture or looking upon their faces.

Once, an old man was carried into the hospital. He was unconscious and unable to breathe.

'If I waste only a few seconds, then he could die.'

Fr. Taesuk instantly looked at the man's face and felt in his bones that the man had malaria. He promptly performed CPR to get his heart beating again. And then immediately, he injected the malaria medicine. After a while, the man regained his consciousness. His family almost jumped up and down for joy over the unexpected result.

"We all believed that he was going to die."

In this way, Fr. Taesuk gradually became a well known doctor.

The clinic work was a demanding and tiring job, but Fr. Taesuk felt it rewarding. The most fruitful thing of all was the fact that more and more people came to believe in Jesus Christ.

Four to five hundred people got baptized every year and the church was crowded every time it had a mass. Fr. Taesuk did not force anyone to come to church. On the contrary, people voluntarily visited the church after experiencing his devoted service. They opened their hearts not because of what he said but because of what he did.

Fr. Taesuk witnessed so many great things. All the people whom he had treated were healed completely and came to church. They turned into faithful believers. They believed in God's love toward them. Some of them hoped to live as Fr. Taesuk. Fr. Taesuk found great pleasure in them and felt rewarded.

Becoming a Teacher - a Planter of Dreams and Hope

Fr. Taesuk still remembered what he had first seen during his visit to Sudan. He remembered the destroyed buildings, people all skin and bones, crawling lepers with crushed limbs, hungry babies crying for food…

'What a miserable place this is!'

His heart was torn with sorrow, never seeing this before in his life. But above all, the most heartbreaking sight was children doing absolutely nothing with their time. They were sitting

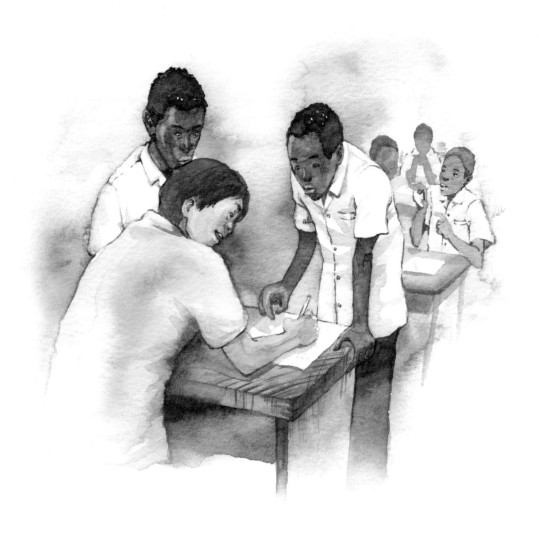

absent-mindedly under trees without any energy to do anything. They had dull eyes which showed no hope for the future.

'It's a tragedy that they don't dream a bright future.'

He wanted to give them hope and dreams. As he returned to Sudan, he set about doing teaching work. He first gathered as many as seventy children, and started to teach them. He used the shadow of the trees instead of classrooms, tree branches and the ground instead of pencils and notebooks. The students were enthusiastic and enjoyed learning. He wanted to provide them with better environments. And so, he built a few small huts, and used them as classrooms. He also made chairs out of logs.

One night, he was taking a walk when some children at a distance greeted him.

"Hello, Father!"

"Hi, guys. What are you doing there?"

He approached them and found out that they were studying under the moonlight. There was no electricity at home, so it was their only alternative. They were far more passionate about learning than he imagined.

'Above everything else, I should offer them environments suitable for studying.'

He came up with a great idea. He used the church and the clinic building which had lights installed. They were perfect places for the children. The only problem was, the lights drew power from solar energy. So he should set a time-limit. He let them use the places as late as nine o'clock, but they always wanted to study more.

"Father, please let us study another thirty minutes."

"Sorry, kids, but we're running out of electricity."

"Please..." they begged him.

"Well, then, I'll let you stay here until nine thirty. Not later than that, OK?"

"Thank you, Father!"

The children jumped for joy. Fr. Taesuk tried to store as

much energy as he could during the day. He had to do some extra work for more storage, but was so happy to give them more time to study. Their hunger for study grew more and more. They cried out, "Another thirty minutes!" So he allowed them to use the buildings until eleven o'clock.

"OK. OK. Use them as much as you like."

He willingly surrendered to their pestering. The self-study soon became their daily work. They had a prayer time before they began studying, and sang "Hail Mary" together at the end. Fr. Taesuk was so fond and proud of them.

Fr. Taesuk helped the children to go to elementary and junior high school. Yet, they were not able to pursue their studies. Unfortunately, there was no high school in or near the village. The closest one was located 120 km away from where they lived. Furthermore, students usually gave up their studies after finishing junior high school because they could not afford it.

Even some who went to high school later returned to the village. They thought that the level of the teachers or of the class was way too low and not what they expected. The teachers would often miss the classes because often they would not get paid.

'I wish to set up a high school.'

Fr. Taesuk had this thought in mind all along although it was not a simple issue at all. Nothing was ready for his plan: money, classrooms, teachers, etc. He felt both burdened and rushed to do something as soon as possible.

'Where there's a will, there's a way!'

He believed that God would help him once he began. The first thing to do was to search for a suitable building. Luckily, he found an unused storage place at an old elementary school building. It had been bombed during wars. He fixed it into a classroom. Then he brought three teachers from Nairobi. Also, he gave the students school uniforms brought from Korea. He wanted them to feel a sense of pride. In addition to that, he made them student ID cards which became their foremost pride and joy. In this way, the first high school of Tonj was established.

Nevertheless, there were still a lot of things in need, especially teachers. Fr. Taesuk decided to teach math himself. He had great fun in teaching since he loved both math and children. Apart from school classes, he tutored them privately. They would visit him at the clinic after grappling with the problems.

"Father, Father, how do I solve this problem?"

He welcomed them anytime they came to see him.

"Let me see... Well, kid, try this way."

"Thank you, Father. Woops, I mean teacher!"

Introducing Music and
Teaching Peace and Smiles

Fr. Taesuk loved music since he was a child. He remembered the times when he had played the organ at the church. Those were the most happiest of times, spending time with Jesus. Music meant comfort and happiness for him.

'These children need music.'

The children of Tonj rarely knew how it felt to be loved. Many had witnessed the death of their parents, brothers and sisters. They had to fight with arms to protect their family and tribe. They found themselves saddened and embittered. And they seemed destined to be poor. They had been hungry since they were born. They suffered from countless unknown diseases. With all this, they could not find comfort from anywhere.

Fr. Taesuk thought of teaching them music. He imagined them being healed by music just as he had been. He wanted them to see that the world was filled not only with the noise of guns and bombs, but also with beautiful music. He wanted them to be filled with dreams and hope instead of anxiety and hatred. He taught them how to play the instruments. He started with recorders, guitars, and an organ. These instruments were relatively easy to get. At first, he was a little unsure if they could follow his lessons since they had never seen these things before.

'Can they follow my lessons?'

Yet, his fears turned out to be nothing. They felt a little uneasy in the beginning, but as time went by, they fell in love with the instruments and the music sound. They gained a pure passion for music. And so they learned it faster than he had expected. They showed rhythmic sense and musical talent unique in the African people. Some of them played the guitar only one day after they learned it. Others showed amazing talents of playing the organ with both hands just one week after the first lesson.

They soon formed a band composed of recorder, guitar, organ, and drum players as well as singers. The band became popular and was invited to perform at a big event held beside the Agangrial River. Seeing the outstanding musical talent of the children, Fr.Taesuk envisioned an even greater possibility-to organize a brass band team. There had never been one before throughout the entire South. Above all, he needed to find the instruments such as the trumpet, trombone, and clarinet. Fortunately, some acquaintances made a donation and he could purchase the instruments. The organized group was rather a big one of thirty-five members in total. The problem was that he

himself had no idea how to play the instruments.

'There is no one else here but me who can teach them.'

He studied the manuals of the instruments and practiced them with a do-or-die attitude. When he was young, he used to take delight in being introduced to new instruments. And he never gave up until he mastered them fully. He did the same as when he was young. With much dedication, he was able to play them in a week, which was almost a miracle. The next thing to do was to teach the group. He set a goal.

'They will play an ensemble within three months.'

The children turned out to be talented way beyond his expectation. They were playing the instruments at the first day of practice. The next day, they began practicing the chant, "Praise the Lord." They performed it with so much ease that it took only four days to have the first ensemble performance. Fr. Taesuk was in tears to hear the celestial sound that the band produced. His heart burst with joy. The children would probably have felt as much thrill and joy as he had in his childhood.

Along with the musical improvement, their facial expressions began to change. They used to look very stern faced, ready for a battle or fight at any moment. They were not used to revealing their emotions; they seldom laughed or cried. And now with music, they laughed with joy, and smiled in appreciation for teaching them music.

Before they knew, hope welled up in their hearts. One day, a boy said to him, "I wish I could melt all the guns and make instruments out of them!" Fr. Taesuk was deeply touched by his words. Here in Tonj, young boys carried the guns from their early childhood. They could very well have killed somebody. This was their devastating reality. Not any more, though. They began to sing songs about hope and a bright future-a doubtlessly meaningful change.

Fr. Taesuk had one of the greatest times in Tonj in travelling with the brass band. A cardinal from Rome was supposed to visit Sudan for two reasons. One was for the 50th anniversary of founding the diocese, and the other was for the consecration of the iron bridge. Fr. Taesuk and the band were invited to the events. They were held in the city of Rumbek located 120 km away from Tonj. Due to poor road conditions, it would take them at least eight hours to get to Rumbeck. The maximum speed that they could run was 15 to 20 km/h.

He took thirty-five band members. All of them had to sit in the back of a truck with all of the heavy instruments. Along the dusty road, their uniforms and faces became covered with dust. Their black faces turned white. Regardless of all the discomforts, the children were excited the whole time. They chattered and sang songs like birds. They were having fun in their first time ever trip.

On the following morning of their arrival in Rumbeck, they skipped breakfast and headed directly toward the airport. There, they participated in the welcoming ceremony for the cardinal. Then they moved to a church. They missed lunch again because they had to be there earlier than the cardinal and everyone else. The next destination was where the consecration would be held, 90 km away from Rumbeck. They got on the truck again, but this time they started to grumble.

"Father, I'm hungry."

"When do I eat? I can't play anymore. I'm starving."

Fr. Taesuk himself did not expect that the schedule would be so tight.

"Kids, I'll buy you good food when we're done with our performance. So hang in there."

When night fell, their performance ended. The children were completely exhausted. Fr. Taesuk felt sorry for them. So he brought them to a fancy restaurant and bought each of them a cold coke. They were fascinated by the little tasty drinks they had never had before. They seemed to forget all the hardship they had so far. At that moment, Fr. Taesuk felt like introducing the band to the foreigners eating at the restaurant.

"This is the brass band from Tonj. Would you like to listen to them play?"

The foreigners got curious about this band of African kids. One by one, they gathered around. They began to play so beautifully. As it was over, everybody stood up and gave an enthusiastic round of applause.

"Wow, they are excellent!"

"Can we ask for another song? Please!"

They insisted that the team should give another performance. A man from the crowd removed Fr. Taesuk's hat and placed a bill in it. Then he handed it around to the people. Bills and coins were piled up in the hat in a moment. Everyone in the crowd said that the performance was too good to listen to for free. Even the owner of the restaurant placed no charge on the drinks. In this way, the trip left the children with unforgettable good memories.

The brass band had a second trip to Kuwasok, 200 km away from Tonj. The members were invited to perform at the welcoming ceremony for the President of South Sudan. They left Tonj the day before the special ceremonial day. They were scheduled to arrive there at night. On their way they saw the river flooding the bridge that they were supposed to cross. As time passed, the heavy rainfall caused the river to overflow even higher. They were about to cross the river by truck when one of its wheels got stuck in a mud pit. They felt rushed. So did Fr. Taesuk.

"Get off the truck and hold the instruments. We'll cross the river one by one."

They placed the instruments on their heads, and went across the river. Fr. Taesuk took caution to avoid any accidents. Fortunately, all of them safely reached the other side of the river.

Then he asked around everywhere to find a truck. And finally with the help of God he got one.

"Thank you, God!"

They all arrived safe and sound. On the next day, they saw over a hundred thousand people gathered at the event. They had never seen that many people before. Likewise, people there looked at them curiously, for the fancy uniforms and instruments attracted their attention. The children had a nervous look on their faces.

"Don't be nervous. Do as you always do," Fr. Taesuk encouraged them.

"Yes, Father!"

The ceremony started. The president waved his hand, and the band started to perform. At that moment, something strange happened. The people were only paying attention to the band, instead of the president. The brass band was the top celebrity of the day, not the president. The members got excited along with the people's fervent responses. As members of the brass band, they took pride in themselves. They gained courage and confidence through this special trip. Fr. Taesuk was more than happy for his members.

Living Out God's Love

For Fr. Taesuk, the saddest thing in all Tonj was that children were falling victims to war. The South needed a lot of soldiers to battle the North. At least one person per family had to enter the military. If there were no young men in a family, any male member should be the replacement instead. This could be a 10-year-old boy or a 60-year-old man.

Manual was a soldier. One day, Fr. Taesuk was working at the hospital when a boy suffering a gunshot wound was brought in. He approached the boy who looked around fifteen. He smelled of alcohol.

"What happened to him?"

"He was standing sentry with another soldier and both of them were drunk…"

The truth was that the other boy on duty, also drunk, had shot him by accident. Fr. Taesuk felt heavy-hearted.

'But he is just a kid.'

Then Fr. Taesuk was shocked to see the boy's eyes. They took on a murderous look and resembled an animal's eyes rather than a human's. The 15-year-old boy had turned into a monster because of the adults. Sudden grief struck Fr. Taesuk.

Manual was in the hospital for two months. He was sulky and silent. He was always alone. He often went to the backyard to watch children playing or studying, or the brass band members performing with instruments. He never came up to them, but just observed them.

One day, he came to Fr. Taesuk, drunk. He sat still in front

of Fr. Taesuk for a while, tears coming from his eyes. Then he burst into crying. Fr. Taesuk let him cry. He was pouring out all the sadness that he had kept for a long time.

"Cry your heart out."

Finally, he stopped and began to tell Fr. Taesuk his past story.

"I regret my past, Father."

He was taken into the army when he was nine. He received gun training and was often beaten by the seniors. He had everything to be scared of, but could not run away from it. He even went to war and killed enemies. All those things were too much for him to handle. Six years in the army transformed him into a strong and wild man. At one point, he promised himself that he would never cry. When things were too hard on him, he drank alcohol. He looked back on his past six years while watching other kids. It hurt him deeply in his heart. He wished he could turn back the clock.

"I wish to live a happy life like them."

That was why he cried in front of Fr. Taesuk.

It grieved Fr. Taesuk to see him unhappy. He was ready to do everything to make himself happy. However, all that he could do was listen carefully to him and pat him on the back while he cried. For Manual, he had never gotten any comfort from any grown-ups. It was for the first time in six years that he was comforted.

Leaving the hospital, Manual made up his mind to start a new life. He received his discharge from the army on condition of getting no pay for the past three months of service. And he landed a new job with some skills he had acquired in the army. He was ready to take the first step for a new life. Way to go, Manual!

South Sudanese had long regarded North Sudanese as their enemies. Too many people of the South lost their lives during the war against the North. They had every reason to hate people from the North. The North resisted the growth of the South with every means possible. South Sudan quickly turned into poor have-nots. So the Southern people disliked the Arabs, or the North Sudanese. The Southern people would not believe Fr. Taesuk when he said that there were good Arabs. On the other hand, Fr. Taesuk fully empathized with them after spending quite some time with them.

One day, Fr. Taesuk had some business and had to go to the North. He took a flight to Khartoum, the capital city of Sudan. Unexpectedly, his way was blocked by the security guards at the airport.

"If you come from the South, you can't enter this country. Go home!"

He begged and begged them, but they did not even blink. Luckily, he ran into an acquaintance among the guards and was able to enter the downtown area. He felt pretty bad, though.

Most of the Northern people were Muslims. The problem

was that the North Sudanese government kept interfering with any religions other than Islam. It built mosques next to churches, or Muslim schools next to Christian schools. It went to all lengths to keep other religions from taking root in their land. Fr. Taesuk could not understand it. He gradually developed an ill-feeling toward the North. He felt the same way as the Southern people.

Still, he changed his mind after having visited a technical institute. It was situated near the region of Darfur. Darfur had a painful history. In 2003 when the North attempted to carry out the Arabicization policy, the natives of Darfur rebelled against it and many of their lives were lost. As a result, Darfur became crowded with a lot of children with no families. In this situation, priests and nuns brought them to the school to teach them skills.

The students were mostly Muslim Arabs. He was reluctant to approach them at first. After a while though, he realized that he was mistaken. They were just the same little kids as those in the

South, or even in Korea. Just like them, these Arab kids were hurt, and needed help. His heart went out to those who were working hard to bring them out of poverty.

'What's the problem with Muslims? They too, are just humans like us.'

Fr. Taesuk realized that it was terribly wrong to desert people in need because of their religion. He made himself a promise that he would embrace and comfort them just as he did the Southern kids.

'There is no discrimination in love.'

"Everything is Good!"

Fr. Taesuk visited Korea once every two years. He usually spent two months there, raising awareness of Sudan and appealing for help. He was even busier doing this than back in Sudan.

October 2008, Fr. Taesuk came to Korea. He had a plan to build a high school in Tonj. So he designed a small music concert for fundraising. He was running to and fro in order to make it a success.

One day, a friend of his said to him.

"Taesuk, you look sick. Your skin looks very dark."

"Really? I think I got sunburned."

"Why don't you have a medical checkup?"

His friend kept persuading Fr. Taesuk, and finally he agreed. Unfortunately, Fr. Taesuk's condition proved to be much more serious than he thought.

"Father, you are not in a good condition," the doctor said.

"Do I have any serious problems?"

"You are in the last stage of colon cancer. Cancer cells have spread throughout your body."

The doctor meant that he could die. Surprisingly enough, he remained calm upon hearing the news.

"But I leave for Africa soon."

"Look, Father. You don't understand. You have to be hospitalized right away."

"But I've got things to do. Digging wells, and building a high school…"

He was more concerned about Tonj than about himself. So he went ahead with his work, keeping his illness secret. He even sang songs at the concert.

Finally, the doctor informed Fr. Taesuk's brother of his illness. When he heard it, his brother tried to stop him from working.

"Taesuk, let's take care of your health, first."

"My brother, I really have to go. My kids are waiting for me in Tonj."

Upon seeing his calmness, his brother wept. Fr. Taesuk wept, too.

"Please Taesuk. It won't take long, and I'm sure they'll understand you."

Fr. Taesuk was hospitalized after all. He received anticancer treatments, as many as sixteen times. It was painful and distressing, but he always welcomed his visitors with a smile.

He did not tell the truth to his mother. He was worried that his mother would be shocked to hear the news. He made her believe that he had already left for Sudan. Yet it wasn't too long when she heard about her son. She came to see her son at the hospital. Upon seeing him, she shed rivers of tears. He went through all kinds of hardships and now he is lying in bed with a severe disease. Fr. Taesuk reassured her with a smile.

"Don't worry, Mom. I'm getting better."

His words put her at ease a little bit. Despite the illness Fr. Taesuk kept company with the orphans of the Salesian Order. He kept doing volunteer work for them because he felt the happiest when with them. But, of course, his family urged him to spend some time recuperating in a better place.

"I do this because I want to."

Even his family could not challenge him any more about what he strongly felt. He brought the children in Tonj to mind.

'Hang in there, Taesuk. You'll see them soon,' he said to himself.

His condition worsened, though. His face turned dark. He suffered weight loss, and his hair began to fall out. He looked just like a cancer patient.

He breathed his last breath at 5 a.m. January 14, 2010. Just before he died and in a coma, he muttered a few words in a low voice. He seemed to be having a talk with someone in his dream. People around him found him in peace. He may have seen St. Don Bosco in this last moment. And he left his last message to the people.

"Everything is good!"

He comforted people even at his last moment.

His funeral mass was held on the 16th of January. He was buried in the Salesian Catholic Saints Cemetery in DamYang, Jeolla-do. Among his possessions were some articles of clothing, toiletries, rosaries he prepared as gifts for the Sudanese kids, and two ten-dollar bills. Those were all he had.

Many people feel sorry and sad at the death of Fr. Taesuk Lee. Some of them even say that he lived an unhappy life. They say so because in their own thinking he ended his painful life living only for people, other than himself. Yet, Fr. Taesuk meant it when he said that his life was full of happiness and joy.

"It is certainly hard to share joy and love with the needy, but in the end it turns into far more joy."

Fr. Taesuk Lee gave up a comfortable life and sacrificed himself for the poor people in Tonj. Still, in exchange for an easy life, he received far greater gifts. He went through moments where he felt God's presence more lively and strongly than any other place in the world. He also witnessed moments where his love worked miracles. He confirmed his faith in those moments that would become the foundation for making a better world. Every moment in Tonj was miraculous and full of joy for Fr. Taesuk.

"My life in Tonj was pure happiness itself."

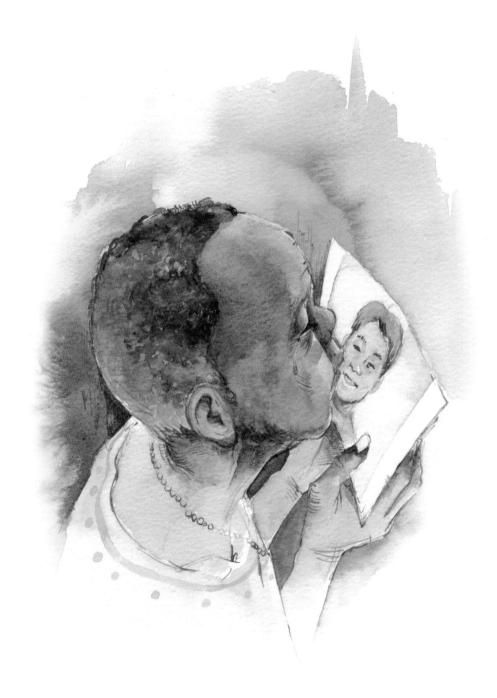

Brother James Kong, an old friend of his, felt like blaming God at first for taking Fr. Taesuk away so early. But now he understands what God intended by his death. Although Fr. Taesuk left this world, the miracles brought forth through him, continue to work.

Fr. Taesuk Lee became known to the public through his biography, *Will you be my friend?* and through the TV documentary program, *Don't cry for me, Tonj.* A lot of people were touched by his acts of love. There are recent movements rising that seek to share the love with others just as he did. *Don't cry for me, Tonj* starts with the narration, "This story is about a man who literally showed that a human being could be a flower for another." Indeed, Fr. Taesuk Lee is remembered as a flower for the people of Tonj. A leper in Tonj kissed the picture of Fr. Taesuk and said, "It is 'tears' to be without him. I feel like crying, as I lay awake at night."

The Salesian Order sent Fr. Kyoung-Min Woo to Tonj to take Fr. Taesuk's place. Fr. Woo is working hard there to build the high school which Fr. Taesuk longed for so badly. Also, the Scholarship Association for the Sudanese Children was established. It is now gaining constant support from all over.

A Sudanese child said, "I want to graduate from high school, and enter college to study medicine. I want to save a lot of people like Father Lee." He passed away, but the love that he left behind took its root. And in Tonj, it is about to bear fruit. His love was worth everything.